THE PREDICTIONS LIBRARY

# GRAPHOLOGY

*David V. Barrett*

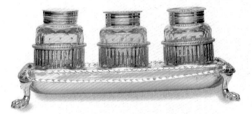

PRENTICE HALL CANADA INC.
SCARBOROUGH, ONTARIO

## A DORLING KINDERSLEY BOOK

*Senior Editor* • Sharon Lucas
*Art Editor* • Anna Benjamin
*Managing Editor* • Krystyna Mayer
*Managing Art Editor* • Derek Coombes
*DTP Designer* • Cressida Joyce
*Picture Researcher* • Becky Halls
*Production Controller* • Sarah Fuller
*US Editor* • Connie Mersel

First Edition, 1995
2 4 6 8 10 9 7 5 3 1

Published in Canada by Prentice Hall Canada
Scarborough, Ontario

A CIP catalogue record for this book
is available from the National Library of Canada

ISBN 0-13-230954-8

Reproduced by Bright Arts, Hong Kong
Printed and bound in Hong Kong by Imago

# CONTENTS

# INTRODUCING
## GRAPHOLOGY

GRAPHOLOGY IS THE STUDY OF HANDWRITING TO REVEAL THE PERSONALITY OF THE WRITER. AN EXPERT GRAPHOLOGIST CAN IDENTIFY MANY CHARACTERISTICS FROM A SINGLE PIECE OF HANDWRITING.

Handwriting is both physiological and psychological. When you write, you use manual skills that are learned and developed throughout your life, but handwriting is also self-expression. A class of children taught the same handwriting style will all develop the style in different ways. By early adulthood, the handwriting of each class member will be unique, showing each individual's personality.

**WRITTEN RULE**
*A very important role for a 15th-century Italian clerk was to write letters and to keep a written record of the ruler's reign.*

than she expected: before she had drunk half the bottle, she found her head pressing against the ceiling, and she stooped to save her neck from being broken, and, hastily put down the bottle, saying to herself "that's quite enough—I hope I shan't grow any more—I wish I hadn't drunk so much!" Alas! it was too late: she went on growing and growing, and very soon had to kneel down in another minute there was not room even for this, and she tried the effect of lying down, with one elbow against the door, and the other arm curled round her head. Still she went on growing, and as a last resource she put one arm out of the window, and one foot up the chimney, and said to herself "now I can do no more — what will become of me?"

**ALICE IN HANDWRITING**
*This original copy of* Alice in Wonderland
*was handwritten by the book's author,
Lewis Carroll (1832–98).*

Many companies request handwritten job applications in order to assess the character of applicants before they are even invited to interview. Graphology has become particularly useful in modern police work. An expert graphologist can point out probable character traits from a single example of handwriting. These traits may help to construct a psychological profile that could help the police in their investigations.

Handwriting is impossible to disguise. Although it is possible to "change" certain signs, a graphologist should be able to spot these attempts at concealment immediately. Graphology cannot, however, reveal the sex, age, or profession of the writer.

# HISTORY
## *of* GRAPHOLOGY

ONE OF THE EARLIEST REFERENCES TO HANDWRITING
WAS BY THE GREEK PHILOSOPHER ARISTOTLE
(384–322 BC), BUT IT WAS NOT UNTIL THE 19TH
CENTURY THAT GRAPHOLOGY BECAME WIDELY KNOWN.

William Shakespeare mentions handwriting in his play *Twelfth Night*. "By my life," cries Malvolio, "this is my lady's hand! These be her very C's, her

U's, and her T's; and thus makes she her great P's. It is, in contempt of question, her hand." (*Act II, Scene V.*) However, Malvolio is wrong; the letter is not penned by Olivia, but by her servant Maria. "I can write very like my lady your niece," she tells Sir Toby Belch, "on a forgotten matter we can hardly make distinction of our hands."

Probably the first book on graphology was written by the Italian doctor and philosopher Camillo Baldo and was published in 1622.

**ROMAN WRITING**
*The Roman historian, Suetonius (c. AD 69–140), included graphological analyses of the Roman rulers in his famous work,* Lives of the Caesars.

GOLDEN GOSPEL
*This mid-8th century English illuminated manuscript is from the* Echternach Gospel Book.

Modern graphology was initially dominated by French clergy. The first school of graphology was founded by Abbé Jean-Hippolyte Michon in 1871. During the 1870s he published two major books on the subject and founded the journal *La Graphologie*, which is still published. His work was extended and consolidated by his pupil Jules Crépieux-Jamin.

The early French work on graphology was based on observation, but the German work in the late 19th century was theoretical and linked graphology with physiology and psychology. At the turn of this century, Dr. Ludwig Klages (1872–1956) began work on one of the most influential developments of graphology, creating a systematic theory linking handwriting with personality. He is perhaps most renowned for realizing that what might be considered a negative sign for one person could be a positive sign for another, and vice versa.

# THE BASIC RULES of GRAPHOLOGY

IN GRAPHOLOGY, THE CONTENT OF THE WRITTEN TEXT
IS ALWAYS IRRELEVANT. FOR EXAMPLE, IN THIS BOOK
HANDWRITING IN SEVERAL DIFFERENT FORMS IS USED,
INCLUDING "LOREM IPSUM" – A TYPE OF FAKE TEXT.

The main differences in the style of handwriting used in a note, love letter, job application, or penmanship practice will be in neatness and spontaneity. The underlying, essential characteristics of the handwriting always remain the same. The analysis of a handwriting sample is likely to be more accurate if it is produced spontaneously, rather than as a penmanship exercise. It also helps the analysis if the sample is written with a Fountain pen, rather than a ballpoint, on unlined paper.

~ 9 ~

When approaching a piece of handwriting for analysis, first take in the overall impression. Graphology has fixed rules, and is often called a science, but your intuition should not be ignored. Is the handwriting neat or messy? How does it sit on the page? Is it large or small, strong or weak? Does it give an impression of boldness or timidity?

~ 9 ~

The graphologist looks at several factors first, before examining the formation of

**ETERNAL ART**
*This Chinese character, Yong, which means "eternal," is the model character for practicing the five basic calligraphic strokes.*

Thương người như thể thương thân!

Thương Người như thể thương thân!

Ghét người như thể đổ phần cho
người.

words and letters. These factors include the margins of the page, the slope of the lines, whether the writing is upright, or slants backward or forward, the size, the rhythm, speed, and flow, the weight and pressure, and the spacing between lines, words, and letters.

~ 9 ~

No individual sign, however apparently clear, should ever be taken on its own as an indication of a character trait. Personalities are multifaceted, and their expression in handwriting reveals this level of complexity, with all its inherent contradictions. The same person can be arrogant yet unsure, or honest yet

## VIETNAMESE HANDWRITING

*Ideally, a handwriting sample should be written with a Fountain pen on unlined paper, like this Vietnamese example.*

cunning. A particular loop or twirl on a certain letter can never ultimately define a person's character.

~ 9 ~

Graphology is an art as well as a science. Graphologists may concentrate on different areas of handwriting, and many have widely differing approaches. However, their assessment of the writer's character is likely to be similar, although they may emphasize different aspects.

# MARGINS

**IF YOUR WRITING IS ON NORMAL UNLINED NOTEPAPER WITHOUT A PRINTED MARGIN, THE SIZE AND REGULARITY OF THE MARGINS GIVE CLUES TO YOUR LEVEL OF INTROVERSION OR EXTROVERSION AND REVEAL YOUR ORGANIZATIONAL ABILITIES.**

I f there is an even margin on the left and right, and a reasonable space at both the top and bottom of the paper, the writer is showing an orderly mind and is taking some care in presentation. Graphologists interpret variations in the margins in slightly different ways, but a wide left margin tends to reveal extroversion, and a narrow

**Left margin becomes wide**

left margin tends to reveal introversion. If the left margin starts normally and becomes wider, it could show a need for more space and independence in the writer's life. If the left margin becomes narrower, it could show a loss of self-confidence, or simply poor planning.

~~~~ 9 ~~~~

A very wide right margin can show self-consciousness, timidity, or a reluctance to face the future. Irregular margins might

**Left margin widens, then narrows**

## Left margin becomes narrow

illustrate a versatile and unconventional mind, but can also show poor self-discipline and a tendency to be unreliable or even unstable.

~ 9 ~

A very wide top margin can indicate caution or hesitancy, but some graphologists also consider it indicative of a generous nature. A very narrow top margin can reveal impatience with other people's restrictions. It can also simply show someone who dislikes any form of procrastination.

~ 9 ~

If all the writing is crammed at the top of the page, leaving an unnecessarily wide bottom margin, it shows a lack of planning and forethought, and possibly a lack of aesthetic awareness. If the bottom margin is almost nonexistent, it can also show a lack of care or planning, or it could indicate the determination of the writer to get his or her thoughts on the page.

~ 9 ~

If the writer fills the paper from top to bottom and from the left edge to the right, it could show a powerful urge to communicate. However, it is just as likely to show a disorderly mind, poor planning, and a lack of respect for the reader. In contrast, very wide margins all the way around the page tend to suggest an inflexible and fastidious nature.

## Irregular left margin

# SLOPE & BASELINE

THE SLOPE OF THE LINE – WHETHER IT IS HORIZONTAL,
ASCENDING OR DESCENDING, CONVEX, CONCAVE,
OR IRREGULAR – REFERS TO THE DIRECTION OR
MOVEMENT OF THE ENTIRE LINE ACROSS THE PAGE.
IT CAN REVEAL OPTIMISM OR PESSIMISM.

Lorem ipsum dolor sit amet, consectetuer adipiscing elit, sed diam nonnummy nibh euismod tincidunt ut laoreet dolore magna aliquam erat volupat. Ut nisi enim veniam, quis nostrud exerci Tation ullamcorper suscipit lobortis nisl ut aliquip ex ea commodo consequat.

If the lines of writing lie straight and parallel across the page, then an upward or downward slope might simply reveal how the paper was positioned. As always in graphology, it is important to look for supporting signs before drawing conclusions. Horizontal lines go straight

### Convex baseline

### Concave baseline

across the page, parallel with the top and bottom. This can show a stable person, or a conformist, or emotional coldness. Ascending lines can show optimism. If individual words rise at their ends, it suggests someone who keeps reaching upward, but lacks the strength to maintain the

Duis autem vel eum iriure dolor in hendrerit in vulputate velit esse molestie consequat, vel illum dolore eu feugiat nulla facilisis at vero eros et accumsan et iusto odio dignissim qui blandit praesent luptatum zzril delenit augue duis dolore te feugait nulla facilisi.

nulla facilisis at vero eros et accumsan et iusto odio dignissim qui blandit praesent luptatum zzril delenit augue duis dolore te feugait nulla facilisi. lorem ipsum dolor sit amet, consectetuer adipiscing elit, sed diam nonummy nibh euismod tincidunt ut laoreet dolore magna aliquam erat volutpat.

effort. Descending lines often show pessimism or depression, but can indicate poor health. If individual words consistently end lower than they begin, the writer may be exhausted or upset.

~~~

Concave lines fall in the middle and rise toward the end. They can show someone who is fighting against depression. Convex lines rise in the middle and slip back down. They indicate a lack of strength or will to maintain any improvement. Irregular

**Meandering baseline**

**Descending baseline**

lines, which rise and fall along their length, usually indicate instability. They can also show intuition and creativity. If the writing stays on the baseline on straightforward horizontal ascending or descending lines, this might reveal consistency and strength of will. If words or letters meander around the baseline, it could show instability and a lack of both self-confidence and sincerity, but it could also indicate a highly versatile mind.

eu feugiat nulla facilisis at vero eros et accumsan et iusto odio dignissim qui blandit praesent luptatum zzril delenit augue duis dolore te feugait nulla facilisi. Lorem ipsum dolor sit amet, consectetuer adipiscing elit, sed diam nonummy nibh euismod tincidunt ut laoreet dolore magna aliquam erat volutpat. Ut wisi enim ad minim veniam, quis nostrud exerci tation

# SLANT

WRITING CAN SLANT FORWARD OR BACKWARD, OR BE
UPRIGHT. THIS CAN BE A USEFUL CLUE TO YOUR
EMOTIONAL STABILITY. HOWEVER, LOOK FOR OTHER
INDICATIONS, BECAUSE SOME CHILDREN ARE TAUGHT
TO WRITE WITH A BUILT-IN SLANT.

Upright writing tends to imply stability and independence – a consistent person with sound judgment. Depending on other indications, however, upright writing could also reveal someone who is cold, or even aloof.

~ ⊙ ~

If the writing slants to the left, it often shows a defensive attitude, and an unwillingness – or perhaps an inability – to reveal or express emotions.

~ ⊙ ~

Handwriting that slants to the right is considered to show a sociable, friendly person, who finds it both interesting and relatively easy to communicate with other people. If the right slant seems to be excessive, it can

**Right slant**

*relit esse molesti*

*et illum dolore eu*

*la facilisis at vero*

*n et inoto odio digna*

suggest a lack of self-discipline, and a tendency to exaggerate emotions.

~ 9 ~

In some countries, children are taught handwriting styles with a built-in slant to the right. The graphologist needs to be aware of such national characteristics, and of the nationality of the writer, so that this can be taken into consideration. Although graphology depends largely on how you unconsciously change your handwriting from the style you were taught, some elements of the original style are still likely to be present.

~ 9 ~

Most writing shows some variation from the overall slant – the occasional letter that moves against the trend. This is quite normal; some irregularity is to be expected, and it can show an element of versatility and imagination.

**Pulling to right and left**

**Left slant**

However, very irregular writing is likely to indicate indecision, confusion, or even aggression.

~ 9 ~

If, in contrast, the slant shows no variation, whether it is upright or left- or right-leaning, it could show someone whose attitude toward life is too fixed and rigid. Such a person is likely to be precise in all aspects of life, and may find it difficult to adapt to the unexpected.

# SIZE

THE SIZE OF HANDWRITING IS RELATIVE. AS WELL AS
NOTING THE OVERALL SIZE, IT IS IMPORTANT TO LOOK
AT THE PROPORTIONS OF THE THREE ZONES OF
HANDWRITING – THE LOWER, MIDDLE, AND UPPER
ZONES – AND THE WRITING'S WIDTH AND HEIGHT.

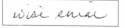

**Small writing**

Graphologists consider writing to be average in size if the middle zone (such as the lower case *o*, *a*, *e*, and *n*, and the circular parts of *b*, *d*, *g*, and *p*) is about ¹⁄₁₆–just under ⅛ in (1.5–2.5 mm) high. Writing is considered small if the middle zone is less than about ¹⁄₁₆ in (1.5 mm) high, and is regarded as large if this zone is just under ⅛ –⅛ in (2.5–4 mm) high. Writing that is more than ⅛ in (4 mm) high is considered very large. If the

writing is very small or large, the graphologist should check that it was affected by no unusual conditions, such as a small piece of paper for a long note, or the need to letter a poster for display. It is useful to have several samples of the same handwriting to assess the writer's usual writing size.

Small writing can mean that the writer has low self-esteem, or is unusually

**Large writing**

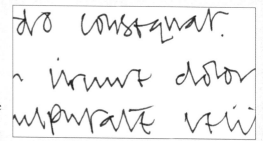

## Tall and thin writing

modest. It could also indicate that the writer has a tendency toward perfection, shows great attention to fine detail, and is patient.

~ ᦆ ~

If the writing starts at a normal size and becomes smaller, either throughout the line or in individual words, it can show sensitivity or diplomacy, but it may also indicate someone whose strength or confidence quickly weakens. It could also simply be a sign of tiredness. If the writing gradually becomes smaller on the entire page, it could mean that the writer is aware of running out of space on the paper.

~ ᦆ ~

Large writing reveals an extroverted personality, generosity, enthusiasm, and an independent mind. It might also be a sign of vanity, or

show a tendency toward domineering leadership. Very large writing almost always indicates these rather negative characteristics. However, check whether either the writer or the recipient of the letter might be partially sighted.

~ ᦆ ~

Writing that becomes larger during a line or a word is usually thought to show naiveté, an almost childlike lack of social judgment or balance, or someone who often exaggerates. It could also be seen as simply showing eagerness and enthusiasm.

~ ᦆ ~

Tall and thin writing shows caution, as well as a restraint that could indicate meanness, but it might also show self-control. Short and wide writing (also known as spaced-out writing) shows a willingness for self-expression and eagerness to communicate.

**Letter size decreases within a word**

# RHYTHM, SPEED, & FLOW

IS THERE A TIGHTNESS IN YOUR WRITING, OR IS IT RELAXED? THE RHYTHM AND SPEED OF YOUR HANDWRITING CAN INDICATE YOUR INNER BALANCE AND THE LIVELINESS OF YOUR THINKING.

**Rhythmic writing**

the middle of a soothing and peaceful symphony.

R hythmic handwriting shows a regular, smooth flow without a self-conscious perfection. If it shows any irregularities, there is almost a pattern to them, as if they have been subconsciously included in the normal flow of the writer's hand. Perhaps the best analogy to consider is a piece of music, whose irregularities form part of an integrated whole. Arrhythmic writing has the effect of harsh discords in

The rhythm of writing shows how "whole" and well-integrated the writer is. In psychological or spiritual terms, the rhythm indicates the balance between the writer's body, mind, and emotions. Graphologists need to be aware of the existence of any physical condition, such as arthritis or cerebral palsy that would affect the

**Arrhythmic writing**

rhythm before drawing conclusions about the writer's inner balance.

~ ⚲ ~

The speed of writing can be recognized by various signs. Slow writing (fewer than 100 letters a minute) often shows careful attention to detail, sometimes with retouching of strokes, which are likely to be quite heavy. Slow writing can simply show slow thinking, but it is just as likely to indicate someone who is thoughtful and reflective. It can also show courtesy to the reader – the writer is working carefully. It could also reveal an unfamiliarity with the language or with the subject matter.

**Slow writing**

**Fast writing**

Fast writing (more than 200 letters a minute) may be recognized by simplified forms of letters, by the pen hardly leaving the paper, and by the i-dots and the t-bars flying to the right and often being linked to the next letter. Fast writing can indicate a lack of care, but is more likely to show quick thinking, enthusiasm, and a mind that is ahead of the hand.

~ ⚲ ~

Although there is a great difference between writing 100 or 200 letters a minute, the variation between these extremes – ranging from calm and controlled to spontaneous and dynamic – is quite wide.

# WEIGHT & PRESSURE

HEAVY PRESSURE TENDS TO SUGGEST INTENSITY AND
LIGHT PRESSURE SENSITIVITY; BOTH CAN HAVE
POSITIVE AND NEGATIVE CONNOTATIONS. VARIATIONS
IN WEIGHT AND PRESSURE AT THE END OF A LETTER OR
WORD ARE PARTICULARLY SIGNIFICANT.

The weight and pressure of handwriting are easier to distinguish if the writer has used a Fountain pen or pencil rather than a ballpoint. It can be very difficult to assess weight and pressure if the graphologist is working from a photocopy rather than the original. With an original, the graphologist can see and feel the pressure. The heaviness or lightness of writing can also depend on the writing surface.

~ ⚬ ~

Heavy pressure could suggest strength

**Heavy pressure**

of will and firmness of intent, or, instead, a bullying and domineering character. Heavy writing tends to show a sensual and perhaps materialistic nature. If the writing flows easily, it shows vitality, and if it does not flow easily, it can show a "heavy" approach to life.

~ ⚬ ~

Light pressure could suggest a weak-willed person, or someone with a deftness of touch. If the writing is well formed it can indicate creativity, adaptability, and sensitivity. If it is not well formed, it could show weakness of body or will, or impracticality.

~ ⚬ ~

"Pasty" writing, which is uniformly thick but without much pressure, can show a warm, sensual, artistic

**Light pressure**

person, but it could also indicate someone who is self-indulgent.

~ 9 ~

There is usually some variation of pressure in a page of writing. A word or phrase that is heavier than the rest of the writing shows an emphasis, whether conscious or unconscious, on the part of the writer. Upstrokes and downstrokes often show different pressure, especially if the handwriting is a variation on a formal style such as italic.

~ 9 ~

If the pressure is even throughout the page, it can indicate a dullness or resignation in the writer. If the writing is simple and shows no intensity, it might

"Pasty" pressure

indicate a personality that is still essentially "unformed."

~ 9 ~

The pressure of the end-stroke of letters and words can indicate the level of aggression in the writer. If the end stroke is sharp and needle-pointed, it can show nervous tension, impatience, and irritability, but depending on other signs, it could also show an incisive mind. If the end stroke is thicker and heavier than the rest of the letter or word, so that it forms a clublike mark, it is likely to indicate brusqueness, strong emotion, or energy that might be misdirected.

# SPACING

THE SPACING BETWEEN THE WORDS IN A SENTENCE IS
RELATED TO THE SENSE OF DISTANCE BETWEEN
YOURSELF AND OTHER PEOPLE. IT CAN SHOW YOUR
LEVEL OF SOCIABILITY, OR YOUR NEED TO HAVE
YOUR OWN PERSONAL SPACE.

> ut aliquip ex ea commodo
> vel eum iriure dolor in h

The normal spacing between words should be between the width of an *n* (or an *a*, *e*, *o*, *u*) and the width of an *m* (or a *w*) in the writer's handwriting. The spacing is narrow if it is less than the width of an *n*. Narrow spacing can show a need to be in the company of other people. Depending on other signs in the writing,

**Narrow word spacing**

**Wide word spacing**

the writer could be a very sociable person with a wide circle of good friends, or insecure, perhaps with a deep fear of loneliness.

If the spacing is wider than an *m*, it can show someone who prefers to keep other people at a distance, both physically and emotionally. Again, the reason for this needs to be judged from other signs. The writer may

> sto odio dignissim qui blan
> m zzril delenit augue du

e feugait nulla faci
psum dolor sit amet
dipscing elit, sed di

be naturally self-sufficient, or be shy and lacking in self-confidence, or be frightened by other people getting too close.

Most people will show a little irregularity in their spacing – at different times everyone needs both solitude and company. If the spacing is very irregular, it could show someone who fluctuates between the two extremes, such as a loner who loves parties, or a normally gregarious person who suddenly becomes quiet and withdrawn.

The spacing between lines reveals similar characteristics. In addition, narrow spacing can show a narrow-minded, closed-in person. Wide spacing can show an isolated person who

**Irregular word spacing**

has difficulty in coping with the world, including other people. Irregular line spacing can show a person with a disorderly mind, who lacks both control and judgment.

congue nihil
d majim plac
orem ipsum
iscing elit, se
euismod tu
magna aliqua

**Wide line spacing**

# STYLE

BEWARE OF MAKING JUDGMENTS THAT DEPEND ON THE ROUNDNESS OR ANGULARITY OF THE LETTERS. FOR EXAMPLE, THE ASSUMPTIONS THAT ROUNDNESS IMPLIES WARMTH AND ANGULARITY SUGGESTS SPIKINESS ARE MORE THAN LIKELY TO BE FALSE.

Handwriting style usually stems from the way you were taught at school. Some schools teach a very simple, rounded hand, where everything is based on the circular letter *o*, others teach a more cursive style, and some still teach a formal italic hand. Fashions in handwriting change; for example, few people, except calligraphers, now write in a copperplate hand.

~ 9 ~

There is now considerably less emphasis on making children produce neat, perfect penmanship, but until recently, many

children were forced into a style of writing that was often at total variance with their personalities.

~ 9 ~

As children grow older and their personalities develop, their handwriting changes. For example, an angular writing style might become more rounded, or a rounded writing style might become more angular. A simple style might become more ornate, or a more complex style might be simplified.

**Italic writing**

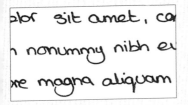

Some stylistic changes are quite deliberate, particularly in the connections between letters, and sometimes in the form of the letters. Loops may be added to the style, or dropped, and innovations such as the flying connection from an *o* to an *l*, or another letter form, might be introduced. Other changes are unconscious, and you might be surprised by the differences between your handwriting five years ago and now, reflecting the gradual changes in your personality over that time.

~ 9 ~

It is more important to look at the changes from the original style than at the style itself. However, an adult who normally writes in a self-consciously perfect hand may be reluctant to change.

**Typical French writing**

## Rounded writing

It is also important for the graphologist to be aware of the writer's country of origin, because there are various national characteristics of handwriting. If someone is writing in an unfamiliar language, the words will be written slowly, precisely, and awkwardly. If someone is writing in the Latin alphabet but their natural tongue is Russian, Greek, or Arabic, their writing is likely to very slow indeed. In this instance, the hesitancy of the writing style, which might usually indicate slowness and dullness of mind, could simply be showing that the writer is unused to writing in the particular alphabet.

# MOOD

IT IS ALWAYS HELPFUL TO HAVE SEVERAL DIFFERENT
WRITING SAMPLES WHEN YOU ARE STUDYING
SOMEONE'S HANDWRITING. IT IS LEAST HELPFUL
TO STUDY A SAMPLE THAT HAS BEEN WRITTEN
EXPRESSLY FOR YOU TO ANALYZE.

Most people will write more neatly in a letter applying for a job than in a letter to a friend. If you are taking notes you might write indecipherably, but if you are handwriting a piece for display, you are likely to write in your most careful style. Any differences in writing style are likely to be variations on the same basic handwriting. Some people claim to have two or three different styles, depending on the purpose of the writing. However, a graphologist should be able to identify different samples of handwriting as having been written by the same person.

It is very helpful for a graphologist to have different examples of someone's handwriting. Different aspects of the writer's personality are likely to

**Display style**

Duis autem vel eum iriure dolore in hendrerit in vulputate velit esse molestie consequat, vel illum dolore eu feugiat nulla facilisis at vero eros et accusman et iusto odio dignissim qui blandit praesent luptatum zzril delenit augue duis dolore te feugait nulla facilisi. Lorem ipsum dolor sit amet, consecteteur adispiscing elit, sed diam nonummy nibh euismod tincidunt ut laoreet dolore magna aliquam erat volutpat. Nam liber tempor cum soluta.

Hallo Luisa,

Vielen lieben Dank für Deine Postkarte. Ich freue mich sehr darauf, Dich im nächsten Monat wiederzusehen! Es ist schon so lange her, seit Du das letzte Mal zu Besuch warst. Bitte teile mir so bald wie möglich mit, wann Du genau ankommst, damit ich Dich vom Flughafen abholen kann. Bis dahin alles Gute und viele Grüße von Deiner

be more apparent in writing done for various purposes. As in everyday life, you reveal some things to strangers and others to friends; sometimes you want to make an impression, and at other times be more modest.

Many people are now aware that if a company asks for a handwritten letter of

**Formal style**

**Informal style**

application, the writing is likely to be analyzed in order to obtain a personality portrait of the applicant. People who know the rudiments of graphology might try to emphasize their positive aspects and suppress their negative aspects. However, an expert graphologist should be able to see through such subterfuge.

Sehr geehrte Damen und Herren,

Bitte schicken Sie mir die letzte Ausgabe Ihrer Zeitschrift "Kunst heute" zur Ansicht. Sollte mich dieses Magazin interessieren, würde ich es in Zukunft gerne abonnieren. Im Voraus vielen Dank.

Mit freundlichem Gruß

# CONNECTIONS

IN HANDWRITING ANALYSIS, ONE OF THE MOST
IMPORTANT AREAS IS HOW THE INDIVIDUAL LETTERS
ARE CONNECTED TO EACH OTHER. THESE
CONNECTIONS CAN REVEAL CONSIDERABLE
INFORMATION ABOUT PERSONALITY.

**Arcade**

a thoughtful, aware
person. Completely
disconnected writing
can show a disorganized
mind, but it could also
show extreme care and
precision, or someone who is
elderly or infirm.

The letters in a word are
rarely all connected. It is
often easier to start a new
letter "clean" than to link it
to the previous letter.
Graphologists usually look
for groups of five or more
connected letters. Partly
connected writing, with
groups of only two or three
letters, is thought to indicate

Graphologists identify four
main ways that letters can be
connected – arcade, thread,
angular, and garland. It is
important to know the
writer's country of origin,

**Thread**

because different countries often have various national characteristics.

Arcade connection arches upward, flying up then down. More connections are made at the top than in garland writing. Arcade writing tends to reveal a consciousness of appearance and effect, but might also show an artistic temperament.

Thread or filiform connection often looks like an unbroken stream of the letters *m* and *w*, in a very loose form. It can show creativity and versatility, but might also indicate laziness, impatience, or a minor illness. Angular connection can reveal a straightforward

**Garland**

**Angular**

personality, as well as firmness, and decisiveness. It tends to point toward someone who prefers logic and facts to intuition.

Garland connection is concave, whether it joins two letters at the bottom or at the top. It usually denotes a highly sociable and gregarious nature, and also sometimes shows an "earthy" rather than a spiritual personality.

33

# THE MIDDLE ZONE

A SINGLE LINE OF HANDWRITING IS DIVIDED INTO
THREE HORIZONTAL ZONES – THE MIDDLE, UPPER, AND
LOWER ZONES. THE MIDDLE ZONE REVEALS HOW YOU
PERCEIVE YOURSELF AND THE VALUE YOU PUT ON
YOURSELF IN RELATION TO OTHER PEOPLE.

The three zones represent (from top to bottom) your aspirations and ambitions, your self and sociability, and your emotional and materialistic aspects. These three zones should always be in balance with each other.

~ੴ~

A zone that is considerably more developed than the others reveals an over-concentration in that area, and a zone that is underdeveloped in comparison with the other zones reveals a weakness in that specific area.

The middle zone consists of the lower-case letters *a, c, e, m, n, o, r, s, u, v, w, x*, and a simple *z*, the rounded parts of the letters *b, d, g, p*, and *q*, and the central parts of *f, h, i, j, k, l, t*, and *y*.

~ੴ~

The middle zone is the center of your writing. It needs to be a strong and firm base for all your hopes, dreams, ambitions, emotions, and desires. The upper and lower zones may contain interesting loops and swirls that catch the eye, but if they are not firmly grounded in the middle zone it could reveal

**The three zones**

a földközi tengerparton ?

a lack of stability, coherence, and practicality in your personality. If you are not comfortable with yourself, this is likely to show in an awkward middle zone that is irregular in size and wanders erratically around the baseline.

~ 9 ~

The middle zone reveals what you think of yourself and how you relate to other people. If the middle zone is tall in proportion to the other two zones, it usually points toward a high level of self-esteem and social self-assurance, but it may also include a measure of vanity or arrogance. If the middle zone is small in proportion to the other

**Small middle zone**

## Wide middle zone

zones, it can indicate a lack of self-esteem. However, a small lower zone could also show someone who is both intellectual and very independent, and who does not need the assistance or acclaim of other people.

~ 9 ~

If the middle zone is wider than it is tall, it tends to show self-confidence in your skills and abilities, but it might also reveal a tendency toward self-indulgence.

# THE UPPER ZONE

THE UPPER ZONE CONTAINS ALL THE ABSTRACT IDEAS
OF REACHING UPWARD AND BEYOND EVERYDAY
EXISTENCE. THESE MIGHT INCLUDE YOUR SPIRITUAL
ASPIRATIONS, ARTISTIC CREATIVITY, INTUITION, HOPES
AND DREAMS FOR THE FUTURE, AND AMBITION.

The upper zone contains the "ascenders," or upper portions of the lower-case letters *b*, *d*, *f*, *h*, *k*, *l*, and *t*, and the dot of the letter *i*.

~ ⌒ ~

If the upper zone is small in comparison with the other zones, it tends to reveal a certain lack of zest for life – someone who passively accepts their place in the world. Although it points toward a lack of imagination and ambition, it also shows practicality and a down-to-earth nature. If the upper zone appears to be chopped off, rather than simply low, it suggests someone who actively denies any element of reaching upward and outward in their life.

~ ⌒ ~

If the upper zone is tall in comparison with the other zones, it shows someone who is striving for something more. The focus is up to them; for example, they may seek to grow in spiritual, artistic, or career areas. Some graphologists consider a tall upper zone to be more connected with idealism than with spirituality. An upper zone that is very tall

**Small
upper zone**

could indicate unrealistic aspirations, or extreme, single-minded ambition.

~ ❂ ~

A thin upper zone can reveal that the writer has difficulty relating to the abstract; such a person is more comfortable with the concrete.

~ ❂ ~

A full, wide upper zone suggests someone who actively expresses the abstract, such as a writer or artist, a storyteller or musician, a deeply spiritual person, or a skillful and habitual liar.

~ ❂ ~

The upper zone should be a natural extension of the middle zone. If it seems stylistically different from the

**Full upper zone**

**Tall upper zone**

middle zone, then the writer's hopes, dreams, and ambitions have no practical basis.

~ ❂ ~

When examining the upper zone, pay particular attention to the formation of the loops of the ascenders (*see page 41*), and to the dots of the letter *i*, and the crossbars of the letter *t* (*see pages 42–43*).

# THE LOWER ZONE

TRADITIONALLY, THE LOWER ZONE REPRESENTS YOUR "EARTHY" SIDE. THIS MIGHT INCLUDE YOUR DRIVES, IMPULSES, LUSTS, PASSIONS, AND BASIC SURVIVAL SKILLS. IT IS THE ZONE OF THE PHYSICAL, THE MATERIAL, THE FIVE SENSES, AND SENSUALITY.

The lower zone contains the "descenders," or lower portions of the lower-case letters *f, g, j, p, q, y,* and *z*. The loops on downstrokes are usually connected with sensuality (*see page 41*).

A lower zone that is small in comparison with the upper and middle zones suggests that the physical side of life is relatively unimportant for the writer. If the lower zone appears weak, it could indicate someone who is out of touch with the realities of life, or someone who is hesitant and timid. A weak lower zone is also likely to show sexual inhibition.

If the lower zone is large in comparison with the other two zones, it suggests that the writer is more concerned with the tangible nature of the real world than with abstract possibilities. Depending on other signs and indications in the handwriting, this could be

**Small lower zone**

velit esse molestie consequat, ve
la facilisis at vero eros et accu
gni blandit praesent luptatum
re te feugait nulla facilisi.

someone who is utterly practical by nature. The shapes of the loops are likely to show whether the "earthy" aspects of the lower zone are expressed in materialism or in sensuality. A large lower zone is likely to reveal someone who is in touch with their emotions and follows their instincts.

~☉~

If the lower zone is disproportionately large, this could show someone ruled by their instincts. Sensuality might become unrestrained lust, appreciation of fine food could become gluttony, and enjoyment of the fruits of life might become greed. On the positive side, it could show great enthusiasm, enjoyment, and physical energy.

**Constricted lower zone**

**Large lower zone**

Lower stalks of letters that are constricted, or end abruptly, indicate a denial of physical expression and show an active distaste for the sensual side of life. Sexually, the writer is likely to be puritanical, rather than simply uninterested.

~☉~

A very irregular lower zone might show someone whose inner nature is highly sensual, but who is repressing at least some of these desires. It might also reveal frustrations, or sexual or health problems.

estie consequ
facilisis at
o dignissim

# ASCENDERS, DESCENDERS, & LOOPS

THE WAY THAT YOU FORM THE STALKS OF LETTERS (KNOWN AS ASCENDERS AND DESCENDERS) AND HOW THEY LOOP TO CONNECT TO THE NEXT LETTER CAN REVEAL YOUR EMOTIONS AND DESIRES.

**Lassos**

Loops can be part of a taught style of handwriting, and when analyzing loops, it is always useful to know the nationality of the writer. For example, ornate cursive writing with many large, flowing loops is more common in France and the United States than in many other countries.

~~~⌾~~~

If the loops appear to be an integral part of a taught style, they are of less importance in graphological analysis. The reverse is equally true. An italic hand, for example, might have no loops, but their absence should not be considered significant.

~~~⌾~~~

Loops that fly out and back like a lasso can show imagination and mental agility, but are also likely to reveal selfishness and vanity. If there is a triangular movement rather than a rounded loop, it can sometimes indicate a desire to dominate and impose control on other people.

**Typical French loops**

**Entanglement**

Wide loops in the ascenders of the *b*, *d*, *l*, and *h* show that emotions are important to the writer and suggest an open mind. Tight, narrow loops indicate emotional repression. A very high loop might reveal vanity.

~ ⚲ ~

If the downstroke, particularly on *g* and *y*, turns into a wide loop, it suggests a sensual nature – an uninhibited enjoyment of beauty, fine food, and sex. Excessive loops, however, could indicate unrestrained lust, gluttony, and greed. If the loop is tightly controlled, it shows self-control and an attempt to restrain these physical desires.

~ ⚲ ~

Descenders that turn to the left, without any loop, tend to show a desire to return to the past. Descenders that should turn to the left (such as the letters *g* and *y*), but turn to the right instead might reveal a considerable need for independence.

**Wide downward loops**

Sometimes the ascenders and descenders become entangled with the line above or below. Entanglement happens with most people's writing, and could be due simply to a lack of concentration. If it happens frequently, it could show anxiety or agitation.

~ ⚲ ~

Little loops within an *a* or *o*, or the middle zone of letters such as *b*, *d*, *g*, and *p*, can suggest discretion if other signs are favorable, or secrecy if other signs are unfavorable. Unnecessary loops in garland connections between letters might indicate selfishness. In slow writing they might indicate materialism or sensuality, and in fast writing they can show superficiality.

# THE I & THE T

THE LETTERS I AND T CREATE A PAUSE IN YOUR
HANDWRITING BECAUSE IT IS USUALLY NECESSARY TO
LIFT THE PEN FROM THE PAPER TO FORM THE DOT OR
THE CROSS STROKE. THEY CAN REVEAL YOUR STATE OF
MIND AND YOUR ATTENTION TO DETAIL.

It is uncommon to dot every *i*, but if no *i* is dotted, this reveals laziness or a refusal to bother with detail. If every *i* is neatly dotted, close to and in line with the tip of the letter, it shows care and precision. If each dot flies off to the right, and if it is more of a small streak than a dot, it indicates fast writing. If the dot links to the next letter, it could be a sign of intelligence and a logical mind. If each dot lies to the left, it might show a lack of care, or sometimes caution.

A circle instead of a dot above the *i* might show untrustworthiness, or immaturity (*see page 47*).

If the crossbar on a *t* is consistently precisely positioned, it shows a careful attention to detail. A low t-bar might signify a feeling of inferiority, and a high t-bar shows imagination and ambition. A short t-bar suggests caution, and a long

**Downward
t-bars**

*tincidunt ut laoreet liquam erat volutpat.*

t-bar indicates energy. An upward t-bar shows considerable enthusiasm and a reaching out for the higher things in life, and a downward t-bar tends to show unhappiness or weariness. A wavy t-bar usually reveals a good-natured, lighthearted person, but perhaps someone who is an escapist.

~ⓖ~

If a t-bar links with the next letter, it often shows an adaptable, logical mind, which can find useful solutions and shortcuts. However, if the t-bar is linked by a triangle it can show stubbornness, purpose-fulness, or a desire to dominate other people. If the writer uses various

**Dots flying to right**

### Upward t-bars

formations of t-bars in different circumstances, this tends to show versatility and creativity; random formations, on the other hand, might indicate a disorganized mind.

~ⓖ~

The t-bar should touch the upright of the *t*. If the t-bar is not connected and lies to the right, it shows an eager, but essentially unrealistic, person. If it lies to the left, it can suggest a slow-thinking person. A t-bar flying above the stalk might show an imagination that is soaring beyond reality.

*ver adipiscing elit, s tincidunt ut laoreet*

# THE SIGNATURE

YOUR SIGNATURE IS A CLEAR STATEMENT ABOUT YOU –
WHAT YOU THINK OF YOURSELF AND HOW YOU WANT
TO BE PERCEIVED BY OTHER PEOPLE. GRAPHOLOGISTS
CAN OBTAIN CONSIDERABLE INFORMATION ABOUT
YOU SIMPLY FROM YOUR SIGNATURE.

**William Shakespeare's
signature**

If possible, a signature should be analyzed with other samples of the person's handwriting. This enables the graphologist to see whether there are any marked differences between the text, which is a means of conveying information, and the signature, which is effectively the trademark of the writer.

The signature should be in harmony with the rest of the writing, both in personal style and in size. If the style of the signature is completely different from the writing style, the writer essentially lies. Many people devise their signature during adolescence.

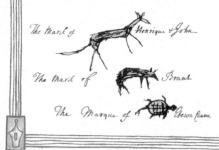

**These 19th-century North American signatures take the form of drawings of animals**

Although their writing develops with their personality, their signature remains fixed, and is therefore no longer a true expression. If the signature is much larger than the rest of the writing, it can show arrogance or perhaps overcompensation for an acknowledged introspective personality. If the signature is smaller than the text, it may reveal low self-esteem.

If the signature is illegible, the writer could be displaying modesty, or devaluing self. In a business letter, an illegible signature is likely to reveal a writer who is too

**Oscar Wilde's signature**

arrogant to bother with clear personal identification. An underlined signature shows firmness and confidence. Two or more lines show a need to be noticed. A wavy

**Beethoven's signature**

line reveals someone who likes to create an effect. A line that crosses through all or part of the signature indicates deep personal dissatisfaction. If part of the name is encircled, or enclosed by the first letter, it suggests protection and defense.

**Underlined signature**

# ELABORATION &
# EMBELLISHMENTS

MANY PEOPLE EMBELLISH THEIR HANDWRITING,
WHETHER IN TEXT OR THEIR SIGNATURE, IN ORDER TO
MAKE THEIR WRITING – AND CONSEQUENTLY
THEMSELVES – APPEAR MORE INTERESTING.

Ornamentation can show vanity or reveal the wish to appear "artistic." Teenagers often create idiosyncratic quirks in their handwriting in an attempt to express their own identity. If such signs remain in adult writing, it can reveal someone who is still trapped in their teenage persona or is projecting a false image. Most elaborations show insincerity and narcissism; the more extravagant the elaboration, the more attention the writer is demanding.

~ ◎ ~

Unnecessarily complicated writing suggests extreme arrogance. If the complexity of the writing obstructs communication, it is ultimately self-defeating.

SOVEREIGN SIGNATURE
*The elaborate signature of Queen Elizabeth I (1533–1603) of England is likely to be a result of an archaic writing style and a queenly haughtiness.*

## SCRIPT WRITING

*The ornate style of writing in this late 16th-century book is known as Chancery script. The book was produced by the Venetian writing expert Giovanni Tagliente.*

One of the most common embellishments is drawing a circle instead of a dot over an *i*. In some countries, such as Spain, this is a common characteristic of handwriting, and reveals personal warmth. However, this embellishment is usually made because the writer thinks that it looks artistic and sophisticated. Unfortunately, it is more likely to reveal immaturity and untrustworthiness.

Arabesques, or flying curves, usually start from the first letter of a word, and reach over part of the rest of the word. They can indicate a patronizing attitude.

Extra, unnecessary loops suggest selfishness. If the writing is slow and steady, extra loops can show sensuality and materialism, and if the writing is fast, they might reveal superficiality.

# HANDWRITING
## ANALYSIS 1

WHEN ANALYZING HANDWRITING, ANY SUBJECTIVE
JUDGMENT MUST BE SUPPORTED BY CAREFUL
ANALYSIS. THIS HANDWRITING SAMPLE IS FROM A
42-YEAR-OLD MAN. IT HAS A PLEASING OVERALL "FEEL."

The left margin becomes wider, showing that this man needs more space in his life. The baseline slopes downward, which might be caused by the paper's position, but some lines descend, others are concave or irregular, and some meander on the baseline. There is also a tendency for words to end lower than they begin. All of these signs suggest depression or tiredness. The attempts to rise at the end of some lines and at the end of some words show the writer's attempts to be positive.

**Sumatran writing
on bamboo strip**

The regular speed and rhythm, upright slant, and even spacing all suggest stability and consistency. The short upper zone shows practicality, which is strengthened by the long descenders of the lower zone.

The pleasing "feel" to the writing suggests that the frequent loops in the letter *o* show diplomacy rather than pretense. The frequent use of unnecessary starting strokes shows dependence, and many of these strokes are arched, indicating reserve. The figure eight in the letter *q* reveals a need to please. The t-bars angle upward, suggesting that the writer is reaching out with enthusiasm. Similarly, the movement to the right of the i-dots shows a strong desire to move on.

STARTING STROKES ARE SLIGHTLY ARCHED AND UNNECESSARY

DESCENDERS OF LOWER ZONE ARE LONG

BASELINE HAS SLIGHT DOWNWARD SLOPE

FREQUENT LOOPS IN THE LETTER O

Lorem ipsum dolor sit amet, consectetuer adipiscing elit, sed diam nonummy nibh euismod tincidunt ut laoreet dolore magna aliquam erat volutpat. Ut wisi enim ad minim veniam, quis nostrud exerci tation ullamcorper suscipit lobortis nisl ut aliquip ex ea commodo consequat. Duis autem vel eum iriure dolor in hendrerit in vulputate velit esse molestie consequat, vel illum dolore eu feugiat nulla facilisis at vero eros et accumsan accumsan et iusto odio dignissim qui blandit praesent luptatum zzril delenit augue duis dolore te feugait nulla facilisi. Lorem ipsum dolor sit amet, consectetuer adipiscing elit, sed diam nonummy nibh euismod tincidunt ut laoreet dolore magna aliquam erat volutpat. Ut wisi enim ad minim veniam, quis nostrud exerci tation ullamcorper suscipit lobortis nisl ut aliquip ex ea commodo consequat. Duis autem vel eum iriure dolor in hendrerit in vulputate velit esse molestie consequat, vel illum dolore

FIGURE EIGHT IN THE LETTER Q

MEANDERING BASELINE

LEFT MARGIN BECOMES WIDER

CONCAVE BASELINE

# HANDWRITING
## ANALYSIS 2

THIS HANDWRITING SAMPLE IS FROM A 26-YEAR-OLD
WOMAN. AT FIRST IMPRESSION, THE SAMPLE IS A
MIXTURE OF FLUIDITY AND ARRHYTHMIC WRITING;
THE WRITING FLOWS, BUT AWKWARDLY.

The thread writing in this sample shows that the writer is more concerned with rapid communication than with making a good impression.

~ 9 ~

The slight irregularity of the left margin within each paragraph might show an unconventional mind, or poor self-discipline. The lines are slightly convex initially, then take on a downward slope, as if the writer has stopped fighting against pessimism – or she could simply be getting tired. Although the slant of the writing is essentially upright, there are also

**Quill-like, steel-nibbed pen**

forward-leaning letters and a persistent pull to the left. This confusion suggests that the woman would like to be sociable, but feels a constant need to be defensive.

~ 9 ~

The word-spacing is wide, suggesting a need to keep a distance from other people. In places, the middle zone is very small in comparison with the other zones. This could suggest that the writer is independent, but it can also show low self-esteem.

~ 9 ~

The stalk height of the *l* and the *d* reveal that the woman wants more in her life. The wide, open curves of the *g* and the *y* show sensuality, but also a desire for security. The t-bar is linked by a triangle, showing purposefulness, or simply stubbornness.

LEFT MARGIN
IS IRREGULAR

LETTERS LEAN
FORWARD

PERSISTENT
PULL TO LEFT

STALK OF D
IS HIGH

Lorem ipsum dolor sit amet, consectetuer adipiscing
elit, sed diam nonummy nibh euismod tincidunt
ut laoreet dolore magna aliquam erat volutpat.
Ut wisi enim ad minim veniam, quis nostrud
exerci tation ullamcorper suscipit lobortis nisl
ut aliquip ex ea commodo consequat.

Duis autem vel eum iriure dolor in hendrerit
in vulputate velit esse molestie consequat, vel
illum dolore eu feugiat nulla facilisis at vero
eros et accumsan et iusto odio dignissim qui
blandit praesent luptatum zzril delenit augue
duis dolore te feugait nulla facilisi. Lorem ipsum
dolor sit amet, consectetuer adipiscing elit, sed
diam nonummy nibh euismod tincidunt ut
laoreet dolore magna aliquam erat volutpat.

Ut wisi enim ad minim veniam, quis nostrud
exerci tation ullamcorper suscipit lobortis
nisl ut aliquip ex ea commodo consequat. Duis
autem vel eum iriure dolor in hendrerit in

51

T-BAR IS LINKED
BY TRIANGLE

LETTERS
DECREASE IN SIZE

CURVE OF G IS
WIDE BUT OPEN

LINES ARE
CONVEX

# HANDWRITING
## ANALYSIS 3

THIS HANDWRITING SAMPLE IS FROM A 21-YEAR-OLD
MAN. THE WRITING IS ARRHYTHMIC AND DISCORDANT,
AND THE PRESSURE IS FAIRLY HEAVY. THE
IRREGULARITY SUGGESTS CONFUSION OR INDECISION.

The very small top margin suggests that the writer always wants to get on with the job at hand. The meandering baseline and the fact that individual words both rise and fall suggests inconsistency and a lack of self-confidence.

~ ⚲ ~

The slant is mainly upright, with some leaning to the right, and an occasional backward pull. The word spacing is wide, suggesting that the writer is uncomfortable when other people get

Chinese characters

too close. The connections of letters within words is erratic, but the writer usually joins only two or three letters, showing awareness.

~ ⚲ ~

The middle zone tends to be smaller than the other two zones. This could show independence and intelligence, or a lack of self-esteem. The upper zone has either simple stalks or very tight, narrow loops, which show that the man prefers the practical to the abstract. Most of the descenders are straight stalks, sometimes with a slight hook instead of a curve or loop. This suggests an intense, narrow focus of concentration, and possibly an attachment to possessions. The wide variety of t-bar formations might show inconsistency, but it can also show versatility.

WORD SPACING IS WIDE

TIGHT, NARROW LOOPS IN UPPER ZONE

MIDDLE ZONE IS SMALLER THAN OTHER ZONES

MEANDERING BASELINE

Lorem ipsum dolor sit amet, consectetuer adipiscing elit, sed diam nonummy nibh euismod tincidunt ut laoreet dolore magna aliquam erat volutpat. Ut wisi enim ad minim veniam, quis nostrud exerci tation ullamcorper suscipit lobortis nisl ut aliquip ex ea commodo consequat. Duis autem vel eum iriure dolor in hendrerit in vulputate velit esse molestie consequat, vel illum dolore eu feugiat nulla facilisis at vero eros et accumsan et iusto odio dignissim qui blandit praesent luptatum zzril delenit augue duis dolore te feugait nulla facilisi. Lorem ipsum dolor sit amet, consectetuer adipiscing elit, sed diam nonummy nibh euismod tincidunt ut laoreet dolore magna aliquam erat volutpat. Ut wisi enim ad minim veniam, quis nostrud exerci tation ullamcorper suscipit lobortis nisl ut aliquip ex ea commodo consequat. Duis autem vel eum iriure dolor in hendrerit in vulputate velit esse molestie consequat, vel illum dolore eu feugiat nulla facilisis at vero eros et accumsan et iusto odio dignissim qui blandit praesen

DESCENDERS ARE STRAIGHT STALKS, WITH SLIGHT HOOK

USUALLY ONLY TWO OR THREE LETTERS ARE CONNECTED

WRITING IS ARRHYTHMIC AND DISCORDANT

DESCENDERS ARE ENTANGLED IN LINE BELOW

# HANDWRITING
## ANALYSIS 4

THIS HANDWRITING SAMPLE IS FROM A 32-YEAR-OLD WOMAN. THE WRITING IS LARGE AND ROUNDED, AND GIVES AN OVERALL IMPRESSION OF UNTIDINESS, BUT ALSO WARMTH AND GOOD NATURE.

The writing seems to fill the page, despite the ever-widening margin and word spacing. The baseline changes throughout the sample; it meanders, suggesting uncertainty and confusion, then slopes very steeply upward. Perhaps this shows a determined optimism and liveliness.

The writing is energetic, but there is also a pull to the left. This suggests that the writer is concealing some of her emotions or is unable to express them. The overall writing size, taken with the other indications, shows an extroverted, enthusiastic

**Decorated paper knife**

personality. Her word spacing is wide, which suits the large writing, but it is also irregular, which might suggest a lack of judgment.

The wide middle zone can show self-indulgence, but in this sample it is more likely to show self-assurance and sociability. Some of the d-stalks form very wide loops, showing a creative ability to express the abstract. The g-stalks curve to the left but do not loop, which suggests a return to the past. The descenders rarely connect to the next letter; this could show a disconnection between the writer's past and future. However, the t-bars reach to the right, and often connect with the next letter, revealing a logical, adaptable mind.

NON-LOOPING G

MIDDLE ZONE
IS WIDE

T-BARS REACH
TO RIGHT

WORD-SPACING
IS WIDE, BUT
IRREGULAR

Duis autem vel eum iriure dolor
in hendreit in vulputate velit esse
molestie consequat, vel illum dolore
eu feugiat nulla facilis at vero eros
at accumsan et iusto odio dignissim
qui blandit praesent luptatum
zzril delenit augue duis dolore
te feugait nulla facilisi. Lorem
ipsum dolor sit amet, consectetuer
adipscing elit, sed diam nonummy
nibh euismod tincidunt ut laoreet
dolore magna aliquam erat volutpat.

Ut wisi enim ad minim veniam, quis
nostrud exerci tation ullamcorper
suscipit lobortis nisl ut aliquip

MARGIN IS
EVER-WIDENING

WRITING
PULLS TO LEFT

WIDE LOOPS
OF D-STALK

LINES SLOPE
STEEPLY UPWARDS

# HANDWRITING
## ANALYSIS 5

THIS HANDWRITING SAMPLE IS FROM A 31-YEAR-OLD
MAN. THE BOLDNESS AND CONFIDENCE OF THIS
WRITING – FAST, RHYTHMIC, AND ENTHUSIASTIC –
IS IMMEDIATELY APPARENT.

The left margin widens smoothly and then narrows. This irregularity can show poor self-discipline, but may also be a sign of a versatile and unconventional mind. The baseline is mainly horizontal, but some lines have a slight upward slope. These are signs of consistency and optimism.

~ 9 ~

The consistent right slant of the writing shows sociability and the desire to communicate. The large size reveals an extrovert, and the width of the writing reinforces the eagerness to communicate. In

**Chinese writing**

most places the wide word spacing is in proportion to the size of the writing.

~ 9 ~

The width of the middle zone naturally varies depending on the letter, but it tends to be full, showing confidence and sociability. The upper zone is proportionate and uncluttered. The lower zone is longer and fuller than the upper zone, indicating that the writer is in touch with his senses.

~ 9 ~

Some loop formations are full and complete, suggesting sensuality, while others are more carefully controlled, suggesting an ability to control the passions. The i-dots fly to the right, and many t-bars point upward and to the right. These signs indicate fast writing, and enthusiasm for life.

I-DOTS FLY
TO RIGHT

SOME LINES
HAVE SLIGHT
UPWARD SLOPE

CONTROLLED
LOOP

MIDDLE ZONE
IS FULL

Lorem ipsum dolor sit amet, consectetuer
adipiscing elit, sed diam nonummy nibh
euismod tincidunt ut laoreet dolore
magna aliquam erat volutpat. Ut wisi
enim ad minim veniam, quis nostrud
exerci tation ullamcorper suscipit
lobortis nisl ut aliquip ex ea
commodo consequat.
Duis autem vel eum dolore eu feugiat
nulla facilisis at vero eros et accumsan
et iusto odio dignissim qui blandit
praesent luptatum zzril delenit augue
duis dolore te feugait nulla facilisi.

LEFT MARGIN
WIDENS
SMOOTHLY,
THEN NARROWS

MANY T-BARS
POINT UPWARD
AND TO THE
RIGHT

LOOP IS FULL
AND COMPLETE

WORD SPACING IS
PROPORTIONATE
TO WRITING SIZE

# HANDWRITING
## ANALYSIS 6

THIS HANDWRITING SAMPLE IS FROM A 54-YEAR-OLD
WOMAN. IT IS NEAT AND PLEASING TO THE EYE, IF
RATHER ORNATE. THE STRONG LEFTWARD SLANT
SUGGESTS DEFENSIVENESS.

The writing may look very level, but close inspection reveals a slight downward slope and several convex lines. These could indicate a very slight depression, tiredness, or poor health at the time of writing.

~ 9 ~

The middle zone is small, especially at the end of words. This could indicate sensitivity, but also that the writer's strength or confidence

**Indian script**

weakens quickly. In comparison with the upper zone, the lower zone is fairly underdeveloped. Some of the descenders are simply unadorned straight lines, showing concentration. The exceptions include the triangular formation of the *f*, which reveals a desire to dominate, and the two forms of *g* – one in a reversed formation with a straight stalk and the other with an aggressive, acquisitive hook.

~ 9 ~

The writing is dominated by the huge flying loops of the letter *t*, and by the oversized capital letters. The t-loops are a stylistic affectation which, although extremely artistic and attractive, demand attention. The whiplike *D* shows a lively but forceful personality.

TRIANGULAR
FORMATION OF F

MIDDLE ZONE
IS SMALL,
ESPECIALLY AT
ENDS OF WORDS

AGGRESSIVE,
ACQUISITIVE
HOOK OF G

STRONG,
CONSISTENT
LEFTWARD SLANT

Duis autem vel eum iriure dolor in hendrerit in
vulputate velit esse molestie consequat, vel illum dolore
eu feugiat nulla facilisis at vero eros et accumsan
et iusto odio dignissim qui blandit praesent luptatum
zzril delenit augue duis dolore te feugait nulla
facilisi. Lorem ipsum dolor sit amet, consectetuer
adipiscing elit, sed diam nonummy nibh euismod tincidunt
ut laoreet dolore magna aliquam erat volutpat.
Ut wisi enim ad minim veniam, quis nostrud exerci
tation ullamcorper suscipit lobortis nisl ut aliqui
ex ea commodo consequat. Duis autem vel illum
dolore eum iriure dolor in hendrerit in vulputate ve
esse molestie consequat, vel illum dolore eu feugia
nulla facilisis at vero eros et accumsan et iusto
odio dignissim qui blandit praesent luptatum zzril
delenit augue duis dolore te feugait nulla facilisi
Nam liber tempor cum soluta nobis eleifend option cor
nihil imperdiet doming id quod mazim placerat facer
possim assum. Lorem ipsum dolor sit amet, consectetuer
adipiscing elit, sed diam nonummy nibh euismod tincidunt

LINE IS CONVEX

REVERSED
FORMATION OF G
WITH STRAIGHT
STALK

HUGE, FLYING
T-LOOP

WHIPLIKE D

# INDEX

# ACKNOWLEDGMENTS

*Artwork*
Anna Benjamin

*Special Photography*
Tim Ridley and Steve Gorton.
Thank you to the British Library.

*Editorial assistance* Martha Swift,
*Picture research* Becky Halls and Ingrid Nilsson,
*DTP design assistance* Daniel McCarthy,
*Antique pens* Phyllis Gorlick King.

*Handwriting Samples*
Anna Benjamin, Kate Benjamin, Charlie Chan, Derek Coombes,
Andrew Coulter, Alison Dawson, Ursula Dawson, Sarah Goodwin,
Colette Ho, Fiona Kerr, Ethel Kovacs, Tracie Lee, Sharon Lucas,
Lucy Marsden, Ingrid Morrissey, Fiona Mulvaney, Tinh Thong Nguyen,
Lourdes Rodriguez, Nicole Selke, Nicola Sentance, William Sentance,
Patrick Schirvanian, Jonathan Stansfield, Martha Swift,
Thomas Thirkell, Peter Williams, Pauline Yacoubian.

*Picture Credits*

Key: *t* top; *c* center; *b* below; *l* left; *r* right

Bridgeman Art Library/Kungl. Biblioteket, Stockholm 11*tr*;
British Library 9*t*, 44*bl*, 47*tr*; ET Archive/Biblioteca Marciana, Venice
4*c*/Collegio de Cambio Perugia 8*bl*; Mary Evans Picture Library 10*bl*, 44*t*;
Hulton-Deutsch Collection 45*cr*, 46*b*; Museum of London 5*c*;
Rex Features Ltd/The Times 45*t*.

61